GOD'S REMNANT

BY

APOSTLE LYDIA R. SMITH

First published by AuthorHouse 05/07/04

ISBN: 1-4184-5921-6 (e-book)
ISBN: 1-4184-4645-9 (Paperback)
ISBN: 1-4184-4643-2 (Dust Jacket)

This book is printed on acid free paper.

CONTENTS

FOREWORD

Apostle Lydia R. Smith, in her ongoing efforts to build the Kingdom of God, is using her first book as a vehicle to bring understanding to the end-time Church about God's Remnant.

Apostle Lydia shares divinely revealed insight concerning how God has always preferred to work with the minority, rather than the majority. She unfolds to us the reason why this will always be our God's chosen path for ushering His Divine Plan into the earth. The Apostle convinces us of this truth by recounting examples found in the Word, using a line-upon-line, precept-upon-precept approach.

As Apostle Lydia takes us into the scriptures, she provokes us to take a closer look at not only the Body of Christ, but at our own lives. She answers the question as to why only a chosen few within any congregation are committed to the work of God. She challenges each of us to ask ourselves the important question, "Who Am I?"

Apostle Lydia R. Smith has been given a revelation on this end-time concept that will revolutionize the church world as we know it.

Pastor Lewis Gurley

INTRODUCTION

Over the years, I have heard many people mention the word ***Remnant***. I even had somewhat of an idea of what the word meant. But it was not until I was traveling to one of my churches in Kingfisher, Oklahoma, that the Lord spoke to me loud and clear concerning this word. He said, "Lydia, I have never used an entire church to carry out my perfect plan. I have always used a ***remnant*** out of the church." He said, "You have been looking to the church for the help that you need, expecting the entire church to help carry out the ***Vision*** that I have given you; when in fact, that is not how I work. Within every church, there is always a ***remnant*** of people."

Over the years, I have found myself stressed out…disappointed because I believed everyone in the church should feel the same way I do about carrying out God's Vision. I placed my attention on the church as a whole----not on that special people God had set apart to help carry out His perfect plan.

Well, as you can imagine, the Word that God spoke to me brought revelation, and a total freedom that I have not experienced as an Apostle in the past three years. Then the Lord moved on my heart to write this book. It is for the many church leaders looking to their entire church for help in implementing their Vision. While seeking out help, I know that they too feel an overwhelming sense of disappointment and pain. It is also for those who are called to assist other leaders in carrying out God's **Vision.** As you read, please ask the Lord to open the eyes of your understanding, and to reveal to you the unveiled truth about His ***Remnant.***

Let's take a look at the word ***remnant.*** The American Dictionary (Noah Webster, 1828) ascribes this meaning to the word ***remnant***: *a residue; that which remains after a part is done, performed, told, or passed; a remaining; yet left.* Now, after every rainstorm, there is left a residue. It does not matter if you have just washed and shined your car-- even if it is only water---there will still be a residue on your vehicle. I use this illustration so that you can get a clear vision of what God wants you to know, and it is this:

Saints, God has always used the leftover residue; He always uses that which remains; and He always places His attention on those left standing, when all else

is said and done.

If you have read this much, then get ready for the

greatest revelation you will ever experience.

Part 1

HE TAKES A PEOPLE OUT OF A PEOPLE

Although God spoke to me and said that He always uses a **remnant,** this does not mean that He has no use for the rest of His people. God knows the make-up of His Creation; that not all are willing, and that not all are obedient.

After the great flood spoken of in Genesis 6 and 7, Noah and his family were the ***remnant*** that God used to refurbish the earth. Now, God did not look down to earth and just decide to come up with this great idea, because of the ungodliness of His people. He recognized that His creation was increasing more and more in sin. His thoughts concerning this produced feelings of regret and wasted time in Him:

> *And the Lord was sorry that He had made man on the earth; and He was grieved in His heart.*
>
> ----*Genesis 6:6*

Now, God was so grieved with mankind, that His only option was to destroy what He had created:

So the Lord said, "I will destroy man, whom I created, from the face of the earth, both man and beast, creeping thing and birds of the air, for I am sorry that I have made them."

----<u>*Genesis 6:7*</u>

All God had on His heart was destruction. He wanted to end what He had begun. In the midst of a perverse generation, however, God was able to find a **remnant.** There was someone He could trust to carry out His plan. He was able to find ***a people inside of a People***:

But Noah found grace in the eyes of the Lord.

----<u>*Genesis 6:8*</u>

WOW!! Why do you suppose Noah found grace? Let's read:

Noah was a just man; perfect in his generation. Noah walked with God.

----<u>*Genesis 6:9*</u>

Noah was a just man. The word just can be defined as honest; also, having principles; Godly; righteous. However, let's stick to this definition of the word just: influenced by a regard to the laws of God; or living in exact conformity to the divine will.

Noah was also perfect in his generation. When we hear the word perfect, we love to use it out of context. Listen to the Webster definition of the word perfect: Complete in moral excellences. This same scripture said

"Noah walked with God." Now you have it! Noah was not just another person. He was a "chosen people". Noah lived in exact accord with the laws of God. Noah lived a life of excellence, and he had a relationship with God. He was one in whom God could put his trust to carry out His plan.

God found **a people in the midst of a people** to complete the **Vision**; and this, my friend, is called a **remnant.**

Even though God destroyed Noah's generation, He is not planning to destroy ours. However, He is looking for **a people inside of a people** to carry out His vision. He wants to take that **remnant**, and through them work His perfect plan.

Pastors, please hear me. God does not expect you to look to the entire church for agreement; nor to look to the church to help complete your mission. He has strategically placed "a people" in your midst who have a heart to serve Him; a spirit that is willing; and a love for you. These are God's **remnant**. When all else fails, they will remain standing. I ask you---Who in Genesis 6, was left standing when all was said and done? NOAH.

Do you remember when Jesus fed the five thousand? I know we have often preached on this; but I want you to look at this scripture very closely.

It wasn't only five thousand that Jesus fed:

Now those who had eaten were about five thousand men, besides women and children.

----*Matthew 14:21*

These women and children had to be associated in some way with the five thousand men. If not all, at least some of them were, leaving us with an undetermined amount of people who were fed. Everything that Jesus did ended with a big result.

The scriptures say that Jesus had a multitude following Him. As they followed, they traveled on foot. When Jesus saw this multitude, Matthew 14:14 reads:

He was moved with compassion for them, and healed their sick.

Jesus was touched by their need for Him. He knew why the Father had sent Him; and that drove Him to continue His mission.

As the day came to a close, the Disciples of Jesus came to Him and said, "The hour is late. Send the multitude away so they can go and buy themselves some food." Listen to the response of Jesus to this:

"They do not need to go away; you give them something to eat."

----*Matthew 14:16*

Immediately, the disciples were faced with an impossible situation. I can almost hear what they were thinking: "We have to give all of these people something to eat?!!…when all we have is five loaves and two fish?!! The eyes of the disciples were on the multitudes, while the eyes of Jesus were on their needs. The disciples reacted and responded in the natural, while Jesus reacted and responded in the Spirit.

Through this whole episode, Jesus never allowed doubt and unbelief to enter His heart. As soon as He heard unbelief from His followers, He moved right along in faith. He did not take the time To rebuke them. He did not take the time to correct them. Jesus never agreed, nor depended on them. He simply said:

"Bring them here to Me" *(speaking of the fish and loaves).*

----*Matthew 14:18*

After they brought the five loaves and the two fish to Jesus, He turned to the multitude, commanding them to sit down on the grass (which brought order). Then He took the five loaves and the two fish. Looking up to heaven, He blessed and broke it, and gave the loaves to the disciples, and the disciples gave to the multitudes:

So they all ate and were filled; and they took up twelve baskets full of the fragments that remained.

----<u>*Matthew 14:20*</u>

Now this is my point: God does not need a crowd to get the job done. God took ***a People out of a people***. God used Jesus, not the disciples. (Spiritually, the disciples were not in a place at that time for God to use them.) He had a ***remnant***. He used the one who had a heart that wanted to serve Him. He used the one who had a Spirit that was willing, and who had a love that was undying. His ***remnant*** was Jesus.

Jesus did not allow anyone or anything to stop His ***Vision.*** He carried on, even if He had to do it by Himself. AMEN!!

Saints, you must know that God loves to take a little and make much. Jesus didn't have to go to the grocery store and buy more food. He used what He had. He did what He was told, trusting the Father completely; and in the end, everyone was satisfied, including the faithless disciples. What your Heavenly Father wants you to know is this: if you will let Him, if you will trust Him, if you will obey Him, He will do the same with you. You can be His ***remnant***, faithfully carrying out the will of the Father in the earth.

Part 2

THERE'S MORE TO BE USED

I hear so many Christians talk about their "calling"; but what I found was that the "callings" were all the same. If you ask the question, "What has God called you to do?" The saints reply would be, "He's called me to preach." Then when you question this, their defenses rise, as if you just stole their new car!

Most believers think that the only calling they have is to preach. This type of mindset causes limitations. Their focus becomes the church, the pulpit, and their Sunday morning message; and anything outside of this realm is not of God. They put themselves in a box, not allowing the Holy Spirit to take them into new venues. They are not allowing the Holy Spirit to give them greater expectations; nor are they permitting themselves to explore the true revelations to which God has called the church.

God has bigger plans for the church. He never intended that we sit behind the four walls of a building; nor grip the pulpit as if to say, "I can't do any more than this." Rather, He has called us to a Holy Calling, which has no limitations.

Now, when we talk about being "called" to preach, let us not use this word without true understanding. Has God called you to preach, or did God "command" you to preach? Throughout the Word of God, you will find a "command" to your call to preach the Gospel. In *Matthew 10:27*, Jesus is speaking to His Apostles (v. 27): *Whatever I tell you in the dark, speak in the light; and what you hear in the ear, preach on the housetops.*

Now, this sounds like a "command." He did not ask them to do it; He did not call them to do it; but instead He "commanded" them to do it.

Let's review another scripture in Luke, chapter nine, in which Jesus was talking about the true cost of discipleship. As Jesus was traveling down the road, someone spoke up and said, "Lord, I will follow you wherever you go." Jesus began to explain how certain creatures have a place to rest; but He neither had a place to rest, nor to lay His head. His point was, "Are you sure you _can_ follow me: Not do you _want_ to follow. In other words, can you handle the Task.

Then Jesus said to another, "Follow me," but listen to this man's reply:

Lord, let me first go and bury my Father.

----*Luke 9:59*

Jesus immediately responded by saying: Let the dead bury their own dead; but you go and preach the Kingdom of God.

----Luke 9:60

Saints, the word "go" is a "command" --not a choice. However, in this passage, we see that the "command" fell on the "call." The command was when Jesus called him to follow Him. Then the excuses came, as if he had a choice ("Let me go and bury my Father"). Jesus responded back with a command, "You go and preach the Kingdom of God." Can you see this? We must understand that we are "commanded" to preach the Word of God.

Now we will take a look at two more scriptures:

For if I preach the Gospel, I have nothing to boast of; for necessity is laid upon me; yes, woe is me if I do not preach the Gospel.

----*I Corinthians 9:16*

Paul did not have a choice. Paul had been given a "command". He knew what was required of him. He said …"for necessity is laid upon me."

What does the word "necessity" imply? American Dictionary (Webster, 1828) gives it the following meanings: *That which must be and cannot be otherwise; irresistible power; compulsive force; indispensableness; unavoidableness; inevitableness.* In other words, Paul was saying that he was "commanded" to preach the Gospel.

Let's look at our last scripture. This scripture, found in *2 Timothy,* Shows us that Timothy, Paul's spiritual son in the faith, was having some fears and struggles. Timothy was missing Paul and was crying, not wanting to continue without him. Although Paul loved Timothy as if he were his own son, and understood his fears, he still had to remind Timothy of his responsibilities as a good soldier in God's army.

You, therefore, must endure hardship as a good Soldier of Jesus Christ. No one engaged in warfare entangles himself with the affairs of this life, that he may please him who enlisted him as a soldier.

----*2 Timothy 2:3-4*

Although Paul brought comfort, he also brought a "command." Now what do you suppose the "command" was? You guessed it--"Preach the Word!"

I charge you, therefore, before God and the Lord Jesus Christ, who will judge the living and the dead at His appearing and His

Kingdom: Preach the Word! Be ready in season and out of season, convince; rebuke; exhort, with all longsuffering and teaching.

----*2 Timothy 4:1-2*

Paul concerned himself with strengthening Timothy in his "calling" so that he would be able to preach as "commanded." Timothy was not simply "called" to preach the Gospel. He was "commanded" to do so. However, Timothy's "calling" was the foundation whereby he would preach the Word of God.

By this time, I know you are probably thinking, "What is she talking about?" Hold on! Let's look at verses four and five: And they will turn their ears away from the truth, and be turned aside to fables.

But you be watchful in all things; endure afflictions; do the work of an evangelist; fulfill your ministry.

----2 Timothy 4:4-5

Timothy was "called" alright; but notice, he was "called" to the ministry of an evangelist. He was "called" to be an evangelist, with the "commission" to Preach Jesus.

Now, if you say that God *called* you to preach, so be it. I am not here to argue with you. I must, however, help bring balance to that *calling*. It is easy to say, "God *called* me to preach." If He did, my question to you is this: Out of what *office* were you "called?"

There are five main *offices* in the church, and these offices all carry the *command* to preach the

Gospel. Let's take a look at the scripture concerning this.

> *And He Himself gave some to be Apostles, some Prophets, some Evangelists, and some Pastors and Teachers....*
>
> ----<u>*Ephesians 4:11*</u>

Timothy preached, but he preached from the *office* of an Evangelist. I preach, but I preach from the *office* of an Apostle. However, as an Apostle, I operate in all five *offices*. Paul preached, but from an *office* of an Apostle, able to preach and teach. I believe you are *called*, Do not, however, put yourself in a box. The *call* is more than simply preaching. I know that I must preach the Word; but I also must build the Kingdom of

God. I am not in a box. Jesus has set the captives free and I am free to explore all the avenues He has for me.

> *But to each one of us, grace was given according to the measure of Christ's gift. Therefore He says: "When He Ascended on high, He led captivity captive, and gave gifts to men."*
>
> ----*Ephesians 4:7-8*

Do you really believe that your only *calling* is to preach the Word?

Well, I want you to stretch your faith. God has called you to a higher *calling*. You can do much more than you could ever imagine. If you don't believe that God will take a little and make much, then you are missing the whole point of this book. It is people like you who don't believe that you are capable of much more, that God is calling to a higher calling; a holy calling. You are the ones He can trust and depend on. You can believe that you are just called to preach. Go ahead....stay in your box....miss out on the fun. I promise you, no one will bother you. But for those of you who see the bigger picture, "Go ahead and come on out of the box!! You are not <u>just</u> <u>called</u> to preach. There is more to you -- more that God has for you.

Don't be the one of whom others will say, "Go ahead! Lift up the flap of that box. There isn't even wrapping paper or ribbons on it. It's not even a gift.....it's just another box.

I encourage you to make a choice to allow the Holy Spirit to take you deeper into the things of God. No more limitations, and no more fears.

Nothing but new revelations. Are you out of the box yet? Well, good!. Now we can see the true gift......and that's you. God wants to use you. You are the one that is going to make a difference. You are His **Remnant**......if you believe that you can do more.

26

Part 111

"WHO AM I ?"

I have read the account in the Bible in which God called a man to do a great work. When he realized the task that was before him, his question to God was, "Who am I?" I can definitely understand his response-- or shall I say, his fears-- because when God unveiled His **Vision** before me, my question was the same...."God, who am I?" This question is not a form of disrespect toward our Creator; it is simply a statement of humility. We see an example of this in Moses.

> *Now Moses was tending the flock of Jethro, his father-in-law, the Priest of Midian; and he led the flock to the backside of the desert, and came to Horeb, the Mountain of God.*
>
> -----*Exodus 3:1*

Moses was already working at the time that God called him. He was busy tending the flock of his father-in-law Jethro. The work God had for Moses was not an issue with Moses, because working was something to which he had grown accustom. No, working was not the problem. The *problem* was the **Vision.** If God had said, "Moses, I want you to gather up some rocks and make me an altar," Moses would have done it without question--maybe even completed it that same day. God, however, had a bigger plan for Moses; a plan that caused him to question his own ability, but put him in position to be infused with God's ability.

God is not interested in what you can do; rather His interest lies in what He can do through you. Let's take a look at the Word of God.

And the Lord said, "I have surely seen the oppression of My people who are in Egypt, and have heard their cry because of their taskmasters, for I know their sorrows.

So I have come down to deliver them out of the hand of the Egyptians, and to bring them up from that land to a good and large land; to a land flowing with milk and honey, to the place of the Canaanites, and the Hittites, and the Amorites, and the Perizzites, and the Hivites and the Jebusites.

Now therefore, behold, the cry of the Children of Israel has come to Me, and I have also seen the oppression with which the Egyptians oppress them.

Come now, therefore, and I will send you to Pharaoh that you may bring My people, the Children of Israel, out of Egypt."

-----*Exodus 3:7-10*

Now God was doing fine, until He made Moses aware of his journey.

Moses had no plans to go back to Egypt -- not now; not later; NOT EVER.

But God said, "Come now, I am sending you, Moses." At that point, I believe fear gripped Moses, and all of his past flashed before him. Can you imagine the thoughts that ran through Moses' head: "Here God wants me to go where I barely made it out alive; and on top of that, tell the King to 'Let My people go'." Moses fixed his attention right on that burning bush, and these three words led him from his ability, to God's ability: ***"WHO AM I?"***

> *But Moses said to God, "WHO AM I, that I should go to Pharaoh and that I should bring the Children of Israel out of Egypt?"*
>
> ----*Exodus 3:11*

Now when God revealed His ***Vision*** to Moses, he saw this huge vision through a "little ole me" mentality, causing it to seem so impossible. He saw the ***Vision*** but could not see God in the equation. This is what each of us must guard against, because God is always in the vision. Even when it looks impossible, it really isn't-- because He is in it. As long as you keep looking at yourself, you will never see God; and you will try to accomplish the impossible with your limited ability...not drawing on His ability. What you must realize is that you are not *in* the vision, rather the vision is in you. God has given you a vision to carry; and it is His ability that will cause it to come to pass.

God used a man who did not think very highly of himself. He had no choice but to trust in God's ability;

and because of it, the Children of Israel were set free. Moses was a ***Remnant***. He was forgotten. Left out in the wilderness to die, he was the residue that would not disappear, that God found useful for the Kingdom. Pharaoh may have forgotten him, but God didn't. Bithiah (Pharaoh's daughter) may have forgotten him, but God didn't. Jochebed (Moses biological mother) may have forgotten him, but God didn't.......and the same goes for you and me.

Many people do not have the faith to believe that you are capable of doing anything for God. People are quick to say that you do not have the ability to do this or that. Often because of their opinion, you do not succeed in reaching a higher level in the natural. It looks like the odds are against you. First of all, you are not popular and well known; your name is not important; you do not have much money; and you cannot get that close to the Pastor. So, who are you? This question not only resounds within you, but in others around you. Just know that within those three little words is an opportunity for God to display through you, the splendor of His Glory, the magnitude of His power, and His inconceivable ability.

When Moses asked God, "WHO AM I?", he was simply expressing his awareness of his frailty to accomplish such an awesome task. It was then that God knew that Moses' dependability would lie on His shoulders.... and God would have it no other way. It is God's ability that counts, and it is His capabilities that will accomplish.

It was good for Moses not to think any more highly of himself than he did. This gave God the opportunity to showcase His awesomeness to Pharaoh, to the Israelites, and finally to the world.

To God, our inability is only a vehicle for His ability, which will eventually bring success. So, "WHO ARE YOU?" Let's go into the Word of God and see.

I Corinthians 1:26-28 For you see your calling, brethren, that not many wise according to the flesh, not many mighty, not many noble, are called But God has chosen the foolish things of the world to put to shame the wise, and God has chosen the weak things of the world to put to shame the things which are mighty;

> *and the base things of the world, and the things which are despised God has chosen, and the things which are not, to bring to nothing the things that are.*

Those three little words, "WHO AM I?" have been answered today. You are the one God has chosen to bring about His in-time purpose in these last days. It is in this type of unique humility that God can be glorified. Who gets all of the glory? He does---and as long as you are willing to decrease, He is willing to increase in you.

"WHO ARE YOU?" You are an expression of true humility. The *Vision* is in you, and your God is in the *Vision*. Move toward the burning bush....the Lord is calling you. "WHO ARE YOU?" You are God's

Remnant of today.

THOSE SAME OLD PEOPLE

Story Written by Lydia Smith

There was once a couple who, over the past few years, had made several visits to a particular church. Each time they would enter the doors, they noticed the same people functioning, as if nothing had changed.

On one particular Sunday morning, they decided to attend a church near their home. During breakfast, as the husband engrossed himself in reading the newspaper, he noticed a picture of the church they had frequently visited in the past. Beneath the picture were the words: "Welcome to a Church Where God is in Control."

The man began to share this bit of information with his wife. Her reply was, "Well, would you like to visit there this morning? We haven't been there in over a year." His answer was immediately, "Well, I don't think so; its going to be the same old thing. Honey, I bet you that Mrs. So-and-So is still at the door greeting people; and Mr. You-Know is still the Usher. I bet they still have that same old lady playing that piano." Well, the wife thought, "His mind is made up, so there is no sense begging him." As the wife, however, began to read the paper, she noticed that her husband had omitted part of the article that provided more detail. She then read aloud these words:

"Welcome to a church where God is in control. We now have a new Children's Church Ministry; a Transportation Ministry; and a New Youth Praise and Worship Team. If you do not have a church home, we welcome you to ours, where we guarantee you will be touched by the power of God."

With great excitement, she said to her husband, "Honey, I really want to go there this morning!! If it's the same old routine, I will never ask you to attend again." Well, he agreed, and off to church they went.

As they pulled into the parking lot, they noticed a lot more cars than usual, but the husband still wasn't convinced. He knew that he would see the same old people doing the same old things, so a few more cars did not move him.

As they entered the doors of the church, who was there to greet them? Sister So-and-So. They looked around until their eyes fell on Brother You-Know; and last, but not least, there was that same old lady sitting at the piano. The man looked down at his wife and whispered softly in her ear, "I told you nothing had changed."

As they made their way down the aisle, they felt a hand guiding them. They turned around, and guess who? Sister So-and-So. She greeted them by name, and told them how much she had missed them, as she proceeded to lead them to a seat. As they sat down, they looked at each other, as if to say, "That's different!"

As service started, they noticed very little seating room left. As the man looked around, he felt glad that they had made it in time to get seats.

The service began with the same old lady playing the piano; but there were other sounds not coming from the piano. So he took a quick look in the direction from which the sounds came, and noticed a young man sitting at a keyboard. He thought, "Huh, that's different!"

As the service opened up, he noticed the same man getting up as in the past. This time, however, the man introduced someone else to open the service. The man thought again, "That's different." He then took notice of the Praise Team coming up on the platform, but it was a younger Praise Team with the same old piano player. This really took him by surprise. He thought, "Now this is *really* different." As the young praise team sang, he had not anticipated how much joy he would experience.

Then came time for offering. Who does he see? Yes, Brother You-Know; but behind Brother You-Know were three other ushers that he did not recognize. By this time, he knew he had to abandon his critical and judgmental attitude. He sat preparing himself for the message, expecting to see the Apostle walk onto the platform. To his amazement -- it was not the Apostle, but one of the many Pastors in the church.

The couple enjoyed the service, and both vowed that they would come again. On the drive home, the man said to his wife, "Honey, this was nothing like I expected. Even though the same people were functioning in their same positions, there was just a different glow about each of them. What was that?" The wife replied, "I don't know. All I know is, I enjoyed myself, and I will be going back."

As the husband prepared for bed that evening, he felt an uneasiness in his heart. He lay in bed, only to quickly jump up. He thought to himself, "Huh! This is interesting."

Still unable to understand what was happening to him, the man decided to walk around the house. He began to reminiscence about the times that he had walked closely with God. He remembered the relationship he had enjoyed with Him. Then he thought about all he was missing, by being out of the will of

God. Suddenly, at that moment, he found himself kneeling in front of his coffee table, with his hands folded, calling on the name of Jesus to save him.

After spending some time on his knees, he got up with a joy that was as if he were still listening to the young praise team. He realized then that Jesus had changed his life. With great excitement and overwhelming joy, he raced back into the bedroom, only to find his wife fast asleep. He thought to himself, "This can wait until morning."

As the man again prepared to sleep, he lay down, only to jump up again! He mused, "This is different. Lord, what is really going on?" After hearing nothing from God, he felt this overwhelming sensation to call the Apostle of that church. He looked over at the clock, which read 1:00 a.m., and reasoned, "This, too, can wait until morning. As he stretched out in his bed, this time his attempt to sleep was successful. He slept like a baby, but as soon as day broke, he awakened his wife and shared with her what God had done. She cried and thanked God for his faithfulness.

As soon as 7:00 a.m. rolled around, the man was on the phone calling the Apostle. The Apostle heard the urgency in his voice, and agreed to meet with him later that day. As he walked into the Apostle's office, he realized that he had no idea why he was there; so he endeavored to share how God had touched his life Sunday night.

As he shared, he thought about the Sunday services. He told the Apostle of the discussion he and his wife had before leaving home that morning. He confessed his shame for judging and criticizing everything; but shared that something had happened to him in the midst of the service. He recognized that day that God was drawing him.

As tears filled his eyes, the man apologized for being so hard on the door greeter, the usher, and the piano player. He said, "I only discussed this with my wife; but I feel horrible. The Apostle looked him in the eyes with such love and compassion, and said, "You are truly forgiven." The Apostle stated, "Mr. Newborn, you like so many others don't understand these people. These people you have mentioned are call God's **Remnant**. These people have been here through the storm and through the rain. When others left, they stayed; when others pulled me down, they lifted me up. When no one gave, they did. These people have a calling that cannot be bought. These people have a calling that cannot fade away. If you tried to get rid of them, it would be to no avail." He smiled, and continued, "God has chosen these people to build His Kingdom. If you were to return in two more years, you would find the same people working just as hard as in the beginning.

Although God sometimes raises them up and moves them out, they still are somewhere building the Kingdom. They have taken a lot of criticism, a lot of abuse; but you will find them standing through it all. I have seen them fall, but quickly get back up. I have seen their pain, but they still would reach out to help someone else in need. I have seen their cuts and bruises, but they bandage themselves and keep on moving. These people, my friend, are God's **Remnant**."

The Apostle continued, "God has placed an unyielding power, an undying love, and an overcoming spirit on the inside of His **Remnant**, and they are not to be messed with. They are friends of God; children of God; and servants of God. He can call on them anytime, anywhere; and all you will hear is, 'Here I am, Lord'." They complain little, and eat much (smile).... of the Word. Their delight is in the law of the Word."

"Mr. Newborn, God never called me to build the Kingdom alone. He has provided the church with a **Remnant** -- a few good people. We have the same vision, the same heart, and a mind that wants to do the will of Him who is sending us. So, as you look, take a good look, because it is in these people that the Glory of God shall be revealed. By the way, Mr. Newborn...you are God's **Remnant**, too."

As the man listened, he felt a love he had never before felt. He stood and shook the Apostle's hand, and thanked him for opening his door. As he drove home, he heard a voice say:

"You thought I had forgotten you;

But I have always been here.

I knew that one day

You would turn back my way.

You see, it was the **Remnant** that I used

To get your attention.

Have you not noticed

That they were all you could mention.

They were heavily on your mind

And thick in your thoughts

And look what happened

----You got caught!---

Part V

"A REMNANT SHALL RETURN"

Throughout the Bible, we see that God has always reserved a **Remnant.** Gathered from among His people, this ***remnant*** carried on the work of God, and served as a lighthouse in a dark and sinful world. Many kings and nations started off obedient to God. They served God wholeheartedly; and because of their obedience to Him, received countless blessings. When, however, they disobeyed and judgment came upon their nation, there was always a small group of people who loved God, and remained faithful to Him. This was the ***Remnant.***

At one time or another, we all get full of ourselves. But the time has come for disobedience to diminish. Time is winding down, and God is looking for a few good people who are willing to carry out His plans.

Most Christians start out with a heart for God; but as they progress, their first love for the Kingdom declines. When this happens, what choice does God have? His Word must still go forth. Because He is not a liar, what He says must come to pass. So who is left for Him to use? Who has not gotten full of themselves?

Who has a willing heart? You know, and I know ------it is His **Remnant**.

This book was not designed to bash any ministries or ministers; but it is for self-examination of your own life. Has your vision gotten so big that all you can see is yourself? Have you made it to the top, only to look down on those left behind? Are you so untouchable, that only a certain clientele can come near you? I don't have the answers to these questions; but you do.

I know that I am God's **Remnant**. I don't have much to offer in myself, but I do have Jesus. I know that He is never untouchable. He is not unloving, and his first love has always been "to please the Father." This is the heart of someone who is a part of the

Remnant. God can trust the **Remnant**, because their heart is to please the Lord.

You will find in the Book of Isaiah, chapter 16, that Isaiah prophecies that because of corruption, Moab and his nation, would fall. Genesis 19:36 helps us to understanding why he is corrupt. Here we see the sin of Lot's firstborn daughter who, in order to preserve the lineage of her father, got her father drunk and slept with him. She conceived a son and named him Moab, causing Lot to be both the father and grandfather of Moab. As a result, Moab was corrupt from conception. What chance did he have to be otherwise? Due to the seed having already been corrupted, it was difficult for Moab to stay on course. The name Moab means seed.

God still blessed Moab, causing him to be a very wealthy man. Moab, however, was an idol worshipper, as well as superstitious. His downfall came because he was a very proud man.

We have heard of the pride of Moab --

He is very proud--

Of his haughtiness, and his pride and his wrath;

But his lies shall not be so.

Therefore, Moab shall wail for Moab;

Everyone shall wail. For the foundation of Kir Hareseth you shall mourn;

Surely they are stricken.

----Isaiah 16:6-7

Now this is a man whom God had blessed with great blessings; but the pride brought him to his knees. Let's read on.

Gladness is taken away,

And joy from the plentiful field;

In the vineyards there will be no singing,

Nor will there be shouting;

No treaders will tread out wine in the

 presses;

I have made their shouting cease.

Therefore my heart shall resound like a

 harp for Moab,

And my inner being for Kir Heres.

And it shall come to pass

When it is seen that Moab is weary on the

high place,

That he will come to his sanctuary to pray;

But he will not prevail.

----*Isaiah 16:10-12*

God had removed His presence from Moab. He was not able to dance or sing his way out of this. God had blessed Moab so that he could be a blessing to others. Instead, he allowed pride to be the ruling force in his life. The same is true with so many leaders today. God has blessed them, but they have somehow forgotten the purpose for the blessings.

God realized that the entire nation of Moab was not at fault, however. He knew that there remained a few good people. Let's look at the last two verses.

This is the Word which the Lord has spoken concerning Moab since that time. But now the Lord has spoken, saying, "Within three years, as the years of a hired man, the glory of Moab will be despised with all that great multitude, and the remnant will be very small and feeble."

----<u>*Isaiah 16:13-14*</u>

God said that the **remnant** would be very small and feeble. When I read this, I asked the Lord to give me revelation of this passage, because I knew there was something He wanted me to see. I looked up the word *small* in the Hebrew, and it means *much; of a truth.* Then the Lord led me to the American Dictionary of the English language (Noah Webster, 1828). Listen to these

60

meanings: *feeble; not bright or strong; imperfect. Small: being of little importance; gentle, soft, unworthy; of little ability.)*

My God!! This blew me away! God is very interested in a *nobody*, because he can make them a *somebody*. He does not need your ability. His is enough. He knows we have flaws and that we don't think very highly of ourselves. Listen, Saints, God can----no, God **desires**-- to use you; but the qualities mentioned above are the ones that you must possess. If I were to put it into one word, it would spell h-u-m-i-l-i-t-y. Some of you started off with this quality. However, somewhere along the way, you started seeing *yourself* in God's *Vision*, rather than seeing God.

Through the teachings of Apostle Paul in Romans, God tells us how we should think about our abilities:

For I say, through the grace give to me, to everyone who is among you, not to think of himself more highly than he ought to think; but to think soberly, as God has dealt to each one a measure of faith.

----*Romans 12:3*

The prophet Elijah cried to God on behalf of Israel because God had rejected them. This rejection came, however, as a result of Israel rejecting God's grace. They killed the prophets and tore down all the altars. Elijah stood before God and said, "Lord, I am the only one left, and they too seek to destroy my life." But it was here that God unfolded His everlasting plan:

Yet I have reserved seven thousand in Israel, all whose knees have not bowed to Baal, and every mouth that has not kissed him.

----*I Kings 19:18*

God was letting Elijah know: "I have a **Remnant**; my work will go on."

It is no wonder that everything looked hopeless to Elijah. He was not seeing God in the Vision----he saw himself in the *Vision.* He thought it was his ability that he had to count on......not God's.

Saints, God has a **Remnant.** His choosing will never be because of your name, your title, or your position. God's choosing is not even based on your works. His choosing is by His grace.

Even so then, at this present time, there is a Remnant according to the election of grace.

----*Romans 11:5*

In this passage, God was very much speaking of the latter day church. But will all answer? NO. Will all be obedient? NO, but God has reserved a people who is willing, no matter what the cost, to carry out ***His Vision***. Today, ask yourself -- Are you God's ***Remnant***? Were you at some point, at one time or another, His **Remnant**? Well, it is not too late. He still wants to build the Kingdom. **Repent and let Him use you in the way that He desires.**

ABOUT THE AUTHOR

Apostle Lydia R. Smith is a powerfully gifted writer. Her behind-the-veil revelation conveys a passion to capture and reveal God's Truth. Her work in the ministry has gained her priceless insight for her writings.

In 1999, she opened Iron Pillar Ministries, Inc. where she trains leaders for ministry. She founded Iron Pillar Bible Training Institute. She is the overseer of 104 Churches in East Africa. with two international Pastors. She has opened Agapeland Learning Center. The *Vision* also includes: Iron Pillar Christian Academy; Drug/ Alcohol Rehab; Home for the Homeless; Women's Crisis; a Financial Institution; and a Senior Citizen High-Rise Complex. Her primary goal:

"To take back dominion in the earth.lt is God's plan for mankind to rule in the earth."

For more information, please contact:

Lydia R. Smith Ministries, 120 North Oak

Street, Chandler, Oklahoma 74834

Telephone: 405/258-5988